AMERICAN NOISE

American Noise

Noise

Campbell McGrath

THE ECCO PRESS

The Ecco Press

100 West Broad Street

Hopewell, NJ 08525

Published simultaneously in Canada by

Penguin Books Canada Ltd., Ontario

Printed in the United States of America

Designed by Marian Bantjes

First Edition

LC Card number: 93-20698

ISBN 0-88001-335-4

ISBN 0-88001-374-5 (pbk.)

The text of this book is set in Trade Gothic

for Elizabeth

ACKNOWLEDGMENTS

Some of these poems first appeared in the following publications.

ACM: "Wild Thing"

Antaeus: "Almond Blossoms, Rock and Roll, the Past Seen as Burning Fields," "James Wright, Richard Hugo, the Vanishing Forests of the Pacific Northwest" and "At the Freud Hilton"

Big Wednesday: "Fire & Ash, Times Square, New Year's Day"

Boulevard: "Two Figures with Heat Lightning in the Sangre de Cristo Mountains"

Gettysburg Review: "Smokestacks, Chicago" and "Sugar Skulls, Oaxaca"

The New Yorker: "Night Travelers"

The New York Times: "Wheel of Fire, the Mojave"

Ohio Review: "Dawn" and "Sunset, Route 90, Brewster County, Texas"

Paris Review: "Wheatfield Under Clouded Sky"

Ploughshares: "Angels and the Bars of Manhattan"

Poetry East: "Blue Tulips and Night Train for Jack Kerouac's Grave," "Rock Falls, Illinois," and "Shrimp Boats, Biloxi"

TriQuarterly: "Ode to the Wild Horses of Caineville, Utah"

"Wheatfield Under Clouded Sky" also appeared in the *Pushcart Prize Anthology: XVII.*

Boxcars and electric guitars; ospreys, oceans, glaciers, coins; the whisper of the green corn kachina; the hard sell, the fast buck, casual traffic, nothing at all; nighthawks of the twenty-four-hour donut shops; maples enflamed by the sugars of autumn; aspens lilting sap yellow and viridian; concrete communion of the cloverleaves and interchanges; psalms; sorrow; gold mines, zydeco, alfalfa, 14th Street; sheets of rain across the hills of Antietam; weedy bundles of black-eyed Susans in the vacant lots of Baltimore; smell of eggs and bacon at Denny's, outside Flagstaff, 4 A.M.; bindle stiffs; broken glass; the solitary drifter; the sprinklers of suburbia; protest rallies, rocket launches, traffic jams, swap meets; the Home Shopping Network hawking cubic zirconium; song of the chainsaw and the crack of the bat; wheels of progress and mastery; tug boats, billboards, foghorns, folk songs; pinball machines and mechanical hearts; brave words spoken in ignorance; dance music from the Union Hall; knots of migrant workers like buoys among waves or beads in the green weave of strawberry fields around Watsonville; the faithful touched by tongues of flame in the Elvis cathedrals of Vegas; wildflowers and anthracite; smokestacks and sequoias; avenues of bowling alleys and flamingo tattoos; car alarms, windmills, wedding bells, the blues.

CONTENTS

I

II

I

The name of the game is rapture.

—Jungle Brothers

WHEATFIELD UNDER CLOUDED SKY

Suppose Gauguin had never seen Tahiti. Suppose the *bêche-de-mer* and
    sandalwood trade had not materialized
and the Polynesian gods held fast in the fruit of Nuku Hiva and the milk-
    and-honey waters of Eiao.
Suppose that Europe during whichever century of its rise toward science
    had not lost faith in the soul.
Suppose the need for conquest had turned inward, as a hunger after
    clarity, a siege of the hidden fortress.
Suppose Gauguin had come instead to America. Suppose he left New
    York and traveled west by train
to the silver fields around Carson City where the water-shaped, salt- and
    heart-colored rocks
appeased the painter's sensibility and the ghost-veined filaments called
    his banker's soul to roost.
Suppose he died there, in the collapse of his hand-tunneled mine shaft,
    buried beneath the rubble of desire.
Suppose we take Van Gogh as our model. Suppose we imagine him alone
    in the Dakotas,
subsisting on bulbs and tubers, sketching wildflowers and the sod huts of
    immigrants as he wanders,
an itinerant prairie mystic, like Johnny Appleseed. Suppose what
    consumes him is nothing so obvious as crows
or starlight, steeples, cypresses, pigment, absinthe, epilepsy, reapers or
    sowers or gleaners,

but is, like color, as absolute and bodiless as the far horizon, the journey
toward purity of vision.

Suppose the pattern of wind in the grass could signify a deeper
restlessness or the cries of land-locked gulls bespoke the democratic
nature of our solitude.

Suppose the troubled clouds themselves were harbingers. Suppose the
veil could be lifted.

ALMOND BLOSSOMS, ROCK AND ROLL, THE PAST SEEN AS BURNING FIELDS

Across the highlands farmers are burning their fields
in the darkness. The fleet, infernal silhouettes of these men
and the owl-swift birds scared up from the chaff
flicker briefly against the silken curtain of flame as we pass,
an image from Goya cast once before our eyes
to be lost as the road swerves up to alabaster
groves of olives and white-knuckled *almendros*.
Hungry, exhausted, driving all night, there are four of us
hunched in the shell of the beaten, graffiti-winged bug
that we scalped for sixty dollars in Berlin,
no shocks, bald tires, a broken starter so that
we have to pop the clutch every time, dashing like fools
through the streets of Amsterdam and Barcelona—
Hank with no accent, Dave with no license
except for his beard, Ed with the box turned all the way up,
playing over and over the only two tapes we have left
since the night of the lurid Basque luau
and street riot in San Sebastian. For whatever reason
we are insanely happy. Wild and lost, speed-mad,
high on the stale bread and cold ravioli we've eaten for days,
giddy with smoke and the echoes of flame leading south,
El Greco fingers of chalk blue and turtledove moonlight
at rest on the soft wool mantillas of distant sierras,
rock and roll working its harmonic convergence,

odor of diesel and wild cherry, almond blossoms
settling like ash to the asphalt—. No. Wait.
It wasn't four. There were three of us left
after Hank stayed behind with that girl in Madrid.
And it was ash. Just there, where the highway
carried the flame's liquid insignia, an ash-blizzard
swirled and impelled itself irretrievably
into the melted tar. It was like a county road in Colorado
I once drove, coming to a place where milkweed
or dandelion spores confounded the air
and fell into the fresh-laid blacktop, embedded there,
fossilized, become the antediluvian kingdom
another era must decode. For us, all of Spain was like
anywhere else, driving the Great Plains or Inland Empire,
Los Banos, Buttonwillow, Bakersfield,
familiar rhythm and cadence of the road,
another car, another continent, another rope of lights
slung the length of the San Joaquin Valley.
I don't know if the rush we felt was culturally specific,
though it was the literal noise of our culture we rode
like Vandals or Moors toward a distant sea,
but that feeling was all we ever desired, that freedom
to hurtle madly against the sweet, forgiving flesh of the world,
urged on by stars and wind and music,
kindred spirits of the night. How the past
overwhelms us, violent as floodwaters, vivid as war.
Now Ed wears a suit and tie, Dave deals used cars
in L.A., "pushing iron," as the salesmen say.
My wife and I walk home from the grocery store
through streets of squirrels and school buses

bathed in late October sunlight, musky odor of paper bags
and fresh cheesebread from the Baltic bakery,
when the smell of someone incinerating fallen leaves
brings back a landscape of orchards and windmills,
the inscrutable plains of Castile and Estremadura.
I don't even know what they were burning out there
but it must have been the end
of the season. The symphony of years glissades
like tractors tracing figure eights across a muddy slope,
sweep and lull of machetes in the sugar fields,
Fiji or Jamaica, places Elizabeth and I have traveled since,
smelled the candied stink of smoldering cane.
But what concerns me most is not so much the smoke,
the resin and ash of human loss,
but rather how glibly and with what myopia
we bore the mantle of individual liberty across the continents,
as if our empowerment entailed no sacrifice in kind,
no weight of responsibility. I guess it was a sign
of the times. That jingoistic, re-election year
a spirit of such complacent self-congratulation reigned
that even Paris seemed a refuge from the hubris.
At the Olympic ceremonies in Los Angeles
they chose to reenact the national epic, westward
expansion, only due to certain staging restrictions
the covered wagons full of unflappable coeds
rolled from west to east, a trivial, barely noticed flaw.
It is America's peculiar gift and burden, this liberation
from the shackles of history. And we were such avatars.
We took what was given and thought, in all innocence,
that the casual largesse we displayed in return

was enough. When we parked for good in Algeciras
we left the doors unlocked, key in the ignition.
You see, the brakes were gone and it wasn't our country.
Immense in the heat-shadowed distance loomed
the glittering, mysterious mountains of Africa,
and though we stood in the very shadow of the Rock of Gibraltar
we never even noticed it. That's how I picture us still,
me and Ed and Dave on the ferry to Tangier,
laughing in our sunglasses, forgetting to look back.

WHEEL OF FIRE, THE MOJAVE

What is this white intensity
swallowing me as the night swallows and now disgorges
only Jonah was rocked and the night
is sorrowful music
but this is something else? What is this absence,
immersion as faith is a kind of immersion,
a thirst for light in the true air?
Look at the sun's jailbreak over the violent
walls. I've driven all night
to find myself here. Look at the gypsum desert,
elements scattered like 7-11s all the way to Death Valley,
the way L.A. reaches into it, one hundred miles or more.

I'm talking about America, the thing itself,
white line unreeling, pure distance, pure speed.

I've driven all night

from fear of the darkness that would seize me if I stopped,
even coffee at a truckstop, even water. Look

at the wraiths of stars,
Buick Electras rusting in the freight meadow.

It is the ghost of the light that moves me.

I'm talking about the half-seen,
dawn and evening, desert orchids,
coyotes coming down to the river to drink.
I'm talking about the thing itself,
what rises in the night like anger or grief,
language-less, blistering and overbrimming
as a river coming down from the mountains
to die in the sinks of rushes and alkali,
the absolute purity of light or intention,
memory of grace, seagulls canting windward
above the Great Salt Lake—
                    the sun, the desert,
the weight of the light is staggering—

until even the flesh of our days falls away,
ash from a cone, fruit from a stone. Even now

when the whirling miraculous
wheel in the sky has risen and vanished at first-light,
gears of a huge engine, starlings
drunk on oxygen—
                    when the wheel
is gone and I am alone with the willows
at the edge of the utterly desolate
Mojave River.

            I've driven all night toward the basin
of angels. I've driven all night without understanding

anything, need or desire, this desert, neon
signs remorseless as beacons.

                    I'm talking about America.

I'm talking about loneliness, the thing itself.

I've driven all night to find myself

here. Look around you,
even now look around you.

Dawn breaking open the days like jeweled eggs,
Joshua trees crippled by this freakish rain of light.

SUNSET, ROUTE 90, BREWSTER COUNTY, TEXAS

Now the light is brass and pewter, alloyed metals solid as amber, allied with water, umber and charnel, lucent as mercury, fugitive silver, chalk-rose and coal-blue, true, full of the skulls and skeletons of moonlight, ash light and furnace light, West Texas whiskey light, bevel light, cusp light, light fall of arches and architectonics, earth light and anchor light, sermon light, gospel light, light that clasps hands with the few and the many, mesa light, saltbush and longhorn light, barbed wire and freight train light, light of the suffering, light of the dusk-fallen, weal light and solace light, graveyard at the crossroads light, flood light, harbor light, light of the windmills and light of the hills, light that starts the dove from the thistle, light that leads the horses to water, light of the boon and bounty of the Pecos, light of the Christ of Alpine, light of the savior of Marathon, Jesus of cottonwood, Jesus of oil, Jesus of jackrabbits, Jesus of quail, Jesus of creosote, Jesus of slate, Jesus of solitude, Jesus of grace.

ANGELS AND THE BARS OF MANHATTAN

for Bruce

What I miss most about the city are the angels
and the bars of Manhattan: faithful Cannon's and the Night Cafe;
the Corner Bistro and the infamous White Horse;
McKenna's maniacal hockey fans; the waitresses at Live Bait;
lounges and taverns, taps and pubs;
joints, dives, spots, clubs; all the Blarney
Stones and Roses full of Irish boozers eating brisket
stacked on kaiser rolls with frothing mugs of Ballantine.
How many nights we marked the stations of that cross,
axial or transverse, uptown or down to the East Village
where there's two in every block we'd stop to check,
hoisting McSorleys, shooting tequila and 8-ball
with hipsters and bikers and crazy Ukrainians,
all the black-clad chicks lined up like vodka bottles on Avenue B,
because we liked to drink and talk and argue,
and then at four or five when the whiskey soured
we'd walk the streets for breakfast at some diner,
Daisy's, The Olympia, La Perla del Sur,
deciphering the avenues' hazy lexicon over coffee and eggs,
snow beginning to fall, steam on the windows blurring the film
until the trussed-up sidewalk Christmas trees
resembled something out of Mandelstam,
Russian soldiers bundled in their greatcoats,
honor guard for the republic of salt. Those were the days

of revolutionary zeal. Haughty as dictators, we railed
against the formal elite, certain as Moses or Roger Williams
of our errand into the wilderness. Truly,
there was something almost noble
in the depth of our self-satisfaction, young poets in New York,
how cool. Possessors of absolute knowledge,
we willingly shared it in unmetered verse,
scavenging inspiration from Whitman and history and Hüsker Dü,
from the very bums and benches of Broadway,
precisely the way that the homeless
who lived in the Parks Department garage at 79th Street
jacked in to the fixtures to run their appliances
off the city's live current. Volt pirates;
electrical vampires. But what I can't fully fathom
is the nature of the muse that drew us to begin with,
bound us over to those tenements of rage
as surely as the fractured words scrawled across the stoops
and shuttered windows. Whatever compelled us
to suspend the body of our dreams from poetry's slender reed
when any electric guitar would do? Who did we think was listening?
Who, as we cried out, as we shook, rattled and rolled,
would ever hear us among the blue multitudes of Christmas lights
strung as celestial hierarchies from the ceiling? Who
among the analphabetical ranks and orders
of warped records and second-hand books on our shelves,
the quarterlies and *Silver Surfer* comics, velvet Elvises,
candles burned in homage to *Las Siete Potencias Africanas*
as we sat basking in the half-blue glimmer,
tossing the torn foam basketball nigh the invisible hoop,
listening in our pitiless way to two kinds of music,

loud and louder, anarchy and roar, rock and roll

buckling the fundament with pure, delirious noise.

It welled up in us, huge as snowflakes, as manifold,

the way ice devours the reservoir in Central Park.

Like angels or the Silver Surfer we thought we could

kick free of the stars to steer by dead reckoning.

But whose stars were they? And whose angels

if not Rilke's, or Milton's, even Abraham Lincoln's,

"the better angels of our nature" he hoped would emerge,

air-swimmers descending in apple-green light.

We worshiped the anonymous neon apostles of the city,

cuchifrito cherubs, polystyrene seraphim,

thrones and dominions of linoleum and asphalt:

abandoned barges on the Hudson mudflats;

Bowery jukes oozing sepia and plum-colored light;

headless dolls and eviscerated teddy bears

chained to the grills of a thousand garbage trucks; the elms

that bear the wailing skins of plastic bags in their arms all winter,

throttled and grotesque, so that we sometimes wondered

walking Riverside Drive in February or March

why not just put up cement trees with plastic leaves

and get it over with? There was no limit to our capacity for awe

at the city's miraculous icons and instances,

the frenzied cacophony, the democratic whirlwind.

Drunk on thunder, we believed in vision

and the convocation of heavenly presences summoned

to the chorus. Are they with us still? Are they

listening? Spirit of the tiny lights, ghost beneath the words,

numinous and blue, inhaler of bourbon fumes and errant shots,

are you there? I don't know. Somehow I doubt we'll ever know

which song was ours and which the siren
call of the city. More and more, it seems our errand
is to face the music, bring the noise, scour the rocks
to salvage grace notes and fragmented harmonies,
diving for pearls in the beautiful ruins,
walking all night through the pigeon-haunted streets
as fresh snow softly fills the imprint of our steps.
OK, I'm repeating myself, forgive me, I'm sure brevity
is a virtue. It's just this melody keeps begging to be hummed:
McCarthy's, on 14th Street, where the regulars drink
beer on the rocks and the TV shows "Police Woman"
twenty-four hours a day; the quiet, almost tender way
they let the local derelicts in to sleep it off
in the back booths of the Blue & Gold after closing;
and that sign behind the bar at the Marlin, you know
the one, hand-lettered, scribbled with slogans of love and abuse,
shopworn but still bearing its indomitable message
to the thirsty, smoke-fingered, mood-enhanced masses—
"Ice Cold Six Packs To Go." Now that's a poem.

JAMES WRIGHT, RICHARD HUGO, THE VANISHING FORESTS OF THE PACIFIC NORTHWEST

At least they died of smoke and age and not some awful, active form
of suicide. To keep sight of the forest for love of the suffering trees;
to damp the black or bitter ashes; not to surrender one's humanity
to callousness or grief: this is the hard part. There was much hardness
in their lives but no bitterness so terrible that what remained
seemed not worth having, no fatal poison in their pure American

wellspring. Where did they find such faith? How could America
retain its luster in eyes familiar with exile and war, the informal
inequalities of the factory floor? Why do the bleached remains
of Montana farms assume the character of barren cottonwood trees,
equal testament to the harshness of the local winter and the hardiness
of the will to endure, what Hollywood likes to call "the human

spirit," though why confine such a universal instinct to humanity?
Why believe it's we alone who suffer? How can the native American
ash and alder and Sitka spruce not possess some inkling of the harsh
truth when serpentine logging roads and clear-cut scars form
the totem shapes of grizzly paws on slopes bereft of trees,
when of the great, fog-shouldered forest so little still remains?

Or does it? In Broadway stalls I've seen their work remaindered,
cut rate and still unsold, disregarded by the very people
they spent their lives extolling, and yet there is more in their poetry

than the ghost of the trees killed for paper. There is more to America
than wastefulness and greed and abuse, which are merely forms
of our inherent human weakness, manifestations of the hardship

we suffer when forced to choose for ourselves. Freedom is a hard
row to hoe, our cross to bear, individually and with whatever remnant
of communal will remains to us, whatever common vision yet informs
our deepest dreams and beliefs, the solitary will or the deeply human
dream of community, this central paradox, so typically American,
between the good of the wood and the rights of individual trees.

For me, they loom like redwoods or Douglas fir, the last big trees
of the endangered forest. The timbre of their voices, their wounded hearts
still large enough for sugar beets and four-door Buicks, all things
    American,
all things of simple dignity. Alone or gathered at the river, what remains
is the democratic song, their rich, vernacular empathy with the people,
a common thread of praise. Jim and Dick, in keeping with this form

I carve your informal names in a Western red cedar, totem-pole tree
of the original Americans, because it is sacred and strong of heart.
What thou lovest well remains distinctly, triumphantly human.

FIRE & ASH, TIMES SQUARE, NEW YEAR'S DAY

Past "Prometheus in Teflon," patron saint of the Rock Center ice dryads
    waltzing their way to fortune & fame;
past NBC, down 50th, snare for a rootless gaggle of zanies whose skulls
    like floral Easter eggs
have been sucked high & dry by "The Days of Our Lives"; past chestnuts
    & knishes playing Radio City;
past the tattered, last-gasp Woolworth's thumbed with the stale print of
    dust & olid fudge,
tables of ski-caps & polyester jumpers, aisles of after-shave, "Attaboy"
    dog snacks, two-for-one mini-vacs,
demented shoppers thronging the discount racks while alone at the steam
    table a woebegone TV set shows
Utah State Police officers flushing outlaw polygamists from their log
    cabin hideout with high-frequency sound waves,
and John & Greg Rice, identical-twin midgets, pitching do-it-yourself
    millionaire real estate deals,
yes you can make it happen, yes you can, yes you can; past *Cats;* past
    rats; past Hawaii Kai;
past the guy offering free evaluations at the Scientology table, the
    benevolent specter of L. Ron Hubbard
risen like a bat-winged umbrella of faith from his humble birthplace in
    Tilden, Nebraska;
past the skewed grate dispensing wild jazz amid the roar of the metal-
    driven dream machinery,

passengers in the shadows like nutmeats in raisin toast stepping forth
between the green I-beams
as the express train roars in and sodden flocks of waxed-paper wrappers
take wing in its wake;
past the rank & file army of the porno arcades, omnivorous host of the
stretch-pants parade,
nighthawks of the twenty-four-hour donut shops, the crippled & cryptic
genies of despair,
town criers, lamplighters, flyboys, skyboys, lunatics & lonewolves & pie-
in-the-sky pilgrims,
needle jerks & junk monkeys, toothless impersonators of Goths &
Visigoths rampaging out into traffic;
past it all and down, at last, down the simmering avenues of lust to the
belly of the beast,
where last night's crowd shimmied & shoved to wow & watch the hot-shot
ball of light drop,
where sparrows parrot the gulls' echolalian idiocies and pigeons coast the
exhausted air as dishwater snow
begins to boil over, or circle in soapy currents, or something altogether
grittier, slick & oiled,
an airborne grime swirling faster & faster, cascading in waves across neon
stars & failed resolutions,
settling on stalled cabs & broken trees struck dumb by grief, overarching
the steeples & moribund statuary,
the electroplate giant huddled fearful in the lee of the sacrificial tree as
the asymmetrical skaters pass:
ash, daughter of fire, the pith of a great conflagration, a mighty will raging
against Prometheus;
fire, mother of ash, slouching toward Manhattan, slowly unlimbering her
vast golden hands.

20

SMOKESTACKS, CHICAGO

To burn, to smolder with the jeweled incendiary coal
of wanting, to move and never
stop, to seize, to use,
to shape, grasp, glut, these united
states of transition, that's
it, that is it,
our greatness, right
there. Dig down the ranges, carve out
rivers and handguns and dumps, trash it,
raze it, torch
the whole stuck-pig of it. Why
the fuck not? Immediately I am flying
past some probably
pickup truck with undeniable motor
boat in tow, a caravan
of fishermen no less, bass and bronze eucalyptus scars,
red teeth of erosion click-clacking
their bitterness. And
the sports fans
coming home through a rain
of tattered pompoms. And the restless
guns of suburban hunters shooting
skeet along the lake. Desire is
the name of every vessel out there, but

I think the wind that drives them
is darker. I think I see
the tiny sails are full of hate
and I am
strangely glad. Don't stop,
hate and learn to love your hatred,
learn to kill and love the killing of what you hate,
keep moving,
rage, burn, immolate. Let the one
great hunger flower
among the honeysuckle skulls
and spent shells
of the city. Let longing
fuel the avenues of bowling alleys and flamingo
tattoos. Let sorrow glean the shards
of the soul's bright jars
and abandoned
congregations. Harvest moon
above the petrified
forest of smokestacks.

NIGHT TRAVELERS

Rising from Newark I see the cars of the homebound commuters assem-
bled like migrating caravans.

Lush as glowworms, gregarious as electric eels in their dusty blue Hondas
and plush Monte Carlos,

they jam the tollways and access roads, flood the exits and passing lanes,
circle the sinuous cloverleaves

until they are nothing but rivers of dun and aluminum and butter-colored
light,

arterial channels of ivory and gold, pythons transmuting the freeway web
to luminous honeycomb.

Now I see the Trojan horses of industry, refineries and loading docks at
Elizabeth.

Now the magic kingdom itself, Manhattan, pathologically lucid on Mid-
summer's Eve,

which according to the book I'm trying to lose myself in as we shudder to
scale the oxygen stairwell

was the optimal hour for witches' transport by broomstick and airborne
bread paddle,

the dancing of mad hags under Venus Mountain, the Wild Hunt's en-
chanted stampede,

covenants and covens, auguries and invocations, henbane, belladonna,
elderberry, hemlock,

as the travelers to Hackensack and Scotch Plains must suffer the runes
and rituals of unemancipated flight,

hubbed enumerations and the tokens of interchange, the ghosts of
    evening loosed from backyard barbeques
as from the window I hear the song of baseball cards in bicycle spokes and
    crickets in the neighbor's lawn,
lost summers of crabgrass, resin of oak leaves, taste of chalk from the
    window screen
as I wait for the sound of my father's car in the driveway, Ford Falcon,
    1963,
as even now I imagine the children are sent to bed with patio voices and
    urn-light of fireflies in jelly-jar sarcophagi,
all the children in all the suburbs, tens of thousands, millions of them
    rising into the air in striped pajamas,
hovering like midget astronauts, tiny inmates in coonskin caps, convict
    stars above a nation of lawn chairs and tinkling ice cubes
and sprinklers whirling like tireless apostles, the beautiful sprinklers
    casting their nets, whispering silver apologies to the dust.
Now the air-nurse is passing out thimbles of whiskey, the pilot has spoken
    of vectors and altitude,
trajectory, velocity, how distance reduces to speed over time, the ways our
    lives reduce
to intervals of burnished light on the freeway, a ritual semaphore of stop-
    and-go traffic, sleepy kisses, radio static,
the invisible jet stream propelling us forward as the past recedes like
    farmland beneath our wings.
There are no spells against this grief, no incantations to bridge the long-
    ings of memory,
days and nights I cherish far better than projected wind speed or nomen-
    clature of root salves.
I don't really know when midsummer falls or sign of nightshade or if the
    moon has risen at all beyond the acetylene clouds,

but I am rising to 31,000 feet and as far as I can see there is nothing but
  darkness
and nothing on this craft but bourbon and water and light the color of
  bourbon and water to ease the fire of our passage.

BLUE TULIPS AND NIGHT TRAIN
FOR JACK KEROUAC'S GRAVE

1

This morning I see you slouched beneath the streetlight
on the corner, passing a bottle of tokay with the winos
from the last welfare dives on Belmont—the Julian,
the Bel-Ray, the Diplomat Hotel—a semaphore of cigarettes
and anachronistic neon, *Transients Welcome*
on the blink in rubific pink italic script.
October. Drizzle of elm trees and solemn flags.
Memories of the railroad earth kicked up on the wind
that squeegees fallen leaves along the back alleys
rich with the cast-off declensions of our lives
as those your workboots hustled down in San Francisco,
making time to the freight yard beneath the bridge,
brakeman's watch and lantern clenched with pride,
hooking up with the Sherman Local, out of Bayshore,
boxcars of flowers on the Southern Pacific.
A train full of flowers, how beautiful! How sad,
I suppose you'd say, another in your folio of worldly sorrows.
How typical, too, of that transcendent country,
California, which I knew long before I ever beheld it
would carry its golden "end of land sadness"
unto the very scrollwork of kelp, knew it

from that early morning run, that train you transcribed
to viniferous, seminal, locomotive myth,
Frisco south to San Jose, Coyote and Gilroy and Carnadero,
the overripe valleys and whale-bodied hills,
gondolas of sugar beets like "the heads of decapitated women,"
migrant workers like buoys among waves
or beads in the green weave of strawberry fields
around Watsonville. It was part of the gift,
what you bestowed, or rather, what I took from you,
vineyards and hoboes, yabyum and alpenglow,
age-specific ecstasies to supplant Thomas Wolfe's inchoate desire,
a postadolescent Golden State of blissful melancholia.
Mostly it was your rapturous vision of America
already blossoming like a train of wild roses in my dreams,
your wanderlust and willingness to dive right in,
to dig its scene, praise and criticize, juke and jive,
to scribe its thousand registers into your speed-fueled screed.
Eventually we found it for ourselves, better and worse
than we'd imagined, and proceeded to plot a maniacal course
from coast to coast, back and forth, Chicago to Yellowknife,
New York to L.A. Once we tried to hop a freight,
just once, at a siding along the blue scimitar of Monterey Bay.
After crouching for hours beside a string of dusty flatcars
watching the chains of beaten silver surf concatenate
and uncouple, we traipsed the weeds back into town
where we squandered the last of our cash on rodeo shirts
embroidered with lassos and crimson roses
like the local *brazeros* wore on Saturday night.
We even rode the bus to Lowell one autumn,
me and Charlie, dutiful pilgrims, to drink a bottle of Night Train

and cast a dozen plastic flowers upon your grave,
a wired bouquet we stole from another tombstone,
the coin of someone else's sorrow, a sacramental offering
like the solar marigolds piled in heaps at the Day of the Dead
to light the soul's return from that other world.
Blue tulips. I doubt the light they shed was strong enough,
though our faith had not yet faltered, we never yet
imagined you might not want to find the way,
not want to risk the peace you sought as sanctuary,
a merciful haven from the torment your life became.
For years we had romanticized your death—"the artist's burden"
or the mysterious reification of some American ideal,
whistling "The Ballad of the Green Berets" to the TV's charade,
a hip riposte to Proust's neurasthenic magic lantern,
an integral part of the package, one indivisible groovy ethos,
so down and out it was cool. To the neo-beatnik faithful
you remained a sacrificial paradigm, an icon bleeding
bebop plasma, a boozy, jazz-infused, Buddhist martyr;
to us a tutelary prodigal, a culture-hero to the bitter end.
In truth, what? A drunk Canuck guzzling bourbon, laughing
aloud at "The Beverly Hillbillies"' slaphappy pantomime of bliss,
paranoid and obese, crushed by a mother's alcoholic love?
No, that sounds too punitive, sounds embittered or betrayed,
when all I can see is the tragedy that underlay
those terminal days like a riptide beneath its ceremonial mask,
a penumbral sitcom called "Passive Suicide,"
starring Fear and Inertia, Loneliness and Self-Loathing,
figures shadowed in the mirror the morning after,
voices I myself have heard in the middle of the night,
in the idiot laugh-track that chorused our tireless years of training,

Olympic hopefuls in the Decathlon of Substance Abuse,
huffing reef on the roof with Mike and Bruce,
tequila and ether, gallon jugs of Canadian Ace, the weeks dissolving
like sugar cubes beneath a swizzle stick, the downhill slide,
an effortless glide to lifesavers for lunch again,
corned-beef hash on the unwashed hot plate,
little green monkeys from the Zombies at the China Doll
chained tail to foot from the tasseled lampshade,
chimneys and decibels, ardent keys, lost notes,
the night's electric violets opening their throats,
sun coming up on bottle rings and diadems, the city
emerging like a hula girl gauzed in river mist and steam,
a beautiful barkeep a-swirl with love beads and shrouds of nicotine.
What was it that drove you away from life, Jack?
What conjured that sea change from rhapsody to fugue?
What lily of desire impelled you to the dark, the rain, the storm?
What were you searching for? A soul? A self or freedom
from yourself? The lost father you reveal at the end of *On the Road,*
who feels wrong, fictionalized beyond your already surrogate
namesakes, though ironic in that it was my own father
who gave me his dog-eared edition from the fifties,
which first set my tread toward your footloose steps.
May the soles of your shoes rest in peace at last. Poor Jack.
Sad Jack. Dead in Florida, of all unlikely places,
a tract home near the lush, suburbanized interior
where Uncle Walt's weird swamp vision had newly arisen
to fuel the frenzy of strip-mall construction
like a cinder-block hurricane breaking loose.
So the magic kingdom claims another victim.

2

That very first summer Charlie and I hit the road together—
this was in college, the U.S.F.L. years;
what chance did Thucydides stand against Thunderbird?—
it was to honor your memory at a testimonial shindig in Boulder,
a ballyhooed assembly for which we forged the papers
to deliver a repossessed Lincoln to Denver,
then hitchhiked up to the big Beat reunion
where your highly marketable tale of woe
was laureled and lamented by goofballs and sadsacks
woozily tooting their own kazoos, a syndicate of bromides,
your decaying cadaver displayed like Lenin in his shoebox
for the shameless to ogle and drool upon. Who will buy
this harlequin's body? Who will cop his crown of thorns?
After two days we bagged the weepy waxworks
to wander the town in a potato-colored monsoon
that jackaled the bearded eco-brigades from their squats,
uprooted the street poets and holistic healers, sleepwalked the mimes
and hash-house dropouts back to their garrets.
When the Deadheads upon whose porch we crashed
evicted us forcibly and without explanation
we packed our gear and hit the highway once and for all,
turning fatefully westward again, into the mountains
that made their belated appearance that morning
with the first ray of sunlight we'd seen since Chicago.
I guess you'd say what happened next was obvious,
predictable, though for us a revelation akin to virgin sod,
a wide-eyed arrival at the wild and woolly final frontier:
dharma-bumming the Colorado high country,

pioneering the KOAs, Lewis-and-Clarking the national parks,
Hansel-and-Gretelling up and back to the Great Divide,
when the elements chimed so perfectly with our vibe
that the bottles of wine some freebooters broke
at the campsite refused to cut our feet. At long last
we had discovered the west, invented it, for all we knew,
like Fremont or Pike or a couple of Columbuses,
like Captain Kirk we were ready and able
to seek out and explore, boldly come, boldly gone,
and we cared not a whit that our New World
was full of golden age adventurers and RV explorers,
nitpicking rangers speaking bureaucratese,
mosquitoes convened in galactic swarms, wily marmots
too clever by half, one in particular that seemed
an evil genius of the genus, pillaging our candy bars,
luring us from the fire with feints and dodges
while his partner thieved the bulk of our deviled-ham sandwiches.
When the Wonder Bread ran out we made do with visions
of solace in the cleft-heart valleys, in the meadows
alive with snowmelt waterfalls among the wild blooms
whose messianic names Robert Hass would know.
Monkshood and pasqueflower. Steamboat Springs and Estes Park.
For three weeks we worked washing dishes in Grand Lake,
slept in the owner's mobile home, cavorted at night
with drunken Australians and beautiful Swedish girls
discovering the U.S.A. I think you get the picture.
Youth, freedom, nature, beauty. A kind of vindication,
the canonization of our reading of the text, your text,
not so much the disembodied poetics as the life itself,
an experiential exegesis, an immersion so thorough

that when at last we hitched back down to Denver,
scraggly beards matted with insect repellent,
it was all we could do to combat the shock waves
that bubbled up before we decompressed,
deep sea divers overcoming the bends.
That evening we hopped a Greyhound home.
I remember the drone, the vibration, the pitchless hum;
chill of the night air changing drivers in Ogallala;
the kid who spilled soda all over our stuff.
Sometime before dawn I opened my eyes
to a solitary blue light in the middle of nowhere,
a rotating beacon amid miles and miles of empty fields,
a lighthouse adrift in the wilds of Nebraska,
an eternal flame for the lost mosaic of the plains,
the scattered tribes and vanished buffalo,
a manifestation of something deeper, a greater spirit, whatever it is
that communicates with us through blue light and emptiness,
through wind in the branches of October trees.
It passed in seconds, however I craned to follow its swath,
but for the next few hours I rode alone that pearly conveyance
imbued with a sense of—what can I call it, grief?
the weight of mortality?—something magnificent and sad,
not mystical or miraculous but sacred and real,
something I think you would have recognized,
and I wished you could have been there to take courage from it,
I wished you could have found it, the blue light
you needed to keep going, to endure your secret agonies,
the light we wanted those sorry plastic tulips to cast,
though it was years too late, and we were way too drunk
to consecrate their glow. Later I concluded it was a rural airport,

a landing field for crop dusters and local stunt pilots.
By then we'd made Omaha, breakfast in the bus station,
some quarrel with the driver about Charlie's ticket.
The world in its intransigence binds us to the summons.
This world, our world of fried eggs and panhandlers,
of autumn maples and distant music and smokestacks
wreathed in fog. But it's too late for sermonizing now,
Jack, too late for brow-beating or lamentation,
too late for this elegy to offer you any tangible consolation,
which I suppose, in truth, was never the point.
There's no more sense in talking to the dead
than to these drifts of fallen leaves consumed by the fire
of their mortal sugars. Better to reach the transient,
the golden, the furiously burning spirits of the living.

II

In my hour of darkness,
In my time of need,
O Lord grant me vision,
O Lord grant me speed.

—Gram Parsons

WILD THING

I will be forever nineteen driving a white Impala convertible down the
Pacific Coast Highway while the radio plays nothing but my favorite
songs.
I will live among the wild men of Borneo, drink boar's blood, watch the
slow dance of planets through my bamboo telescope.
I will alter the consciousness of the free world, shake the philosophical
foundations of Western civilization while dating Vanna White.
I will rock the Roxy and the Ritz, ride the rails, roam center field for
the Cubs.
I will rise and shine, I will reign, I will rule, believe me.
Alas, life is poor preparation for death.
All those years of practice for the grand event that never happens,
no flute recital before the masses, no squash game with God.
In such matters our shortsightedness is fundamental.
History is a wave and we surf it beautifully,
carving the face, shredding the curl of that perfectly marbled breaker
spiced with essential stoke. Or so we imagine.
But before this wave came others, and beyond it lies
a veritable ocean of rills and wavelets and mighty tsunamis
we've failed to notice, our eyes so full of spray,
blinded by the tingling sensations of the moment,
as if time were a force field or energized aura,
a second skin, like gravity or desire,
that by its very nature constricts our vision, contains us

as a pig's intestine stuffed with pork and anise
by some overwrought Italian butcher. How else
could Elizabeth continue to wear those shoes,
those black-buckled high tops, combat boots for elves,
which will so clearly seem an utter embarrassment
in the photo album twenty years from now?
My god, look what I wore in the 90s!
How else to explain the statue of Ceres atop the Board of Trade,
elegantly appropriate but left without a face, unfinished,
because they didn't think the city would grow tall enough to notice?
And don't we all recognize that blank expression?
Don't we each cherish our unique and individual nature,
every paper cut or broken heart the first, the most severe,
each vow or resolution the mark of some brave new beginning?
No two snowflakes are exactly alike
but every fucking snowflake is pretty much the same,
every life a variation on a theme of suffering and meaninglessness,
full of distractions—frisbees, beautiful trees,
girls in orange sandals—in fact the distractions
are the main event, there is no grace period,
no warm-up tosses or preseason schedule,
the game has not only begun it's the top of the sixth inning
and you still haven't scored. A shutout.
The world has pitched a shutout against your life.
For all your slick manipulations of that magic bat
you're deep in the hole, the count's against you,
your net result is a fat string of goose eggs
hung like loops of fresh kielbasa from the rafters.
And time is running out, we're into the seventh,
now it's the eighth and the lights are coming on,

the fans are clapping with nervous anticipation.
Look, out in the bullpen, he's warming up:
the main man, the big guy, the stopper, the ace.
But what about those dreams, your hopes for the future—
to plumb the depths of the Marianas Trench in a gilded bathysphere,
to write the epic masterwork of greed and heroism and love,
to build a house with your own two hands in the hills outside of Santa Fe
and raise up chickens and dogs and a family there,
the jet ski, the guitar lessons, the macrame? Hey,
I'd better get serious, get something going before it's too late.
It is too late. Bottom of the ninth. Two gone.
They've given the signal and he's entering the game,
he's coming in to face you, he's making his way slowly across the grass.
The inexorable closer is coming, believe me,
it isn't Mitch Williams.

SUGAR SKULLS, OAXACA

for Gram Parsons

A craft precise as lunar occlusion, slow
cleaved lobe of the cranial
eclipse, vatic
engine borne aloft like ash or song
upon the limbs of Joshua,
sacrament of rock
and roll, liquid silver, solid
gold, honey
on the slide to sweet
solution, high and lonesome
pedal steel. Nothing like this
procession of hearts and candled crosses,
dance of the skeletal mariachis, *gran*
fandango y francachela de todas
las calaveras, un-
sunlight and ur-mirrors,
chicken bones the moon casts out like dominoes or evil
spirits, prefiguration of the needle,
tiny tombstones to mar the delicate
flesh of our throats. Nothing
so momentous as chordal progression,
wavelength escalating toward crescendo, wheel
of fire, pillar of salt,
column that marks the soul's

ascension, the moment
when the guitar goes
voiceless, deft
harmonics in an alien
tongue. Cradle the fret, spike the arc
until it coils like a wicked six-
string lick, stroke the music's
cobbled skin, scaled like fifth notes
and luckless armadillos
flayed to stitch your honky-tonk vestment,
the glyphed and sequined
offices of your dependency. Now
begin the systolic
induction. Match the wick
and clock the boil. Stipple powder to the lip,
stir the copper kettle, pour
the yielded tallow
to the mark. Stay the dye
with milk or oil, boil
ink to scroll
in skirls and hollow links
along the cheeks, strop
the razor,
cinch the fob,
plunge the mold in cold to crack
the seam and free another
bald occipital victim of his crutch.
Hush. Close the lid
to find an inner cosmic
order, heaven and earth

shaken to froth. Feel
the smoky flag
unfurl like etherized horses,
memory of waves
the desert
harbors in pinnacles and ambient
moorings, the unbound
hair of a naked woman kindled
in the vein, eyes
as raven as any ember, her
tattooed arms as beautiful as flames.

NAGASAKI, UNCLE WALT, THE ESCHATOLOGY OF AMERICA'S CENTURY

Like all good stories it starts with a bang: August 6, 1945.
Little Boy, Oppenheimer's aleph, Hiroshima, the bomb.
America's Century begins in fire and ends,
like any respectable act of creation, in something
resembling ash, Alamogordo to Ragnarok, Genesis
to Nagasaki, the black rain wherein we are forever united
with those whose bones we jellied to magma,
siblings minutely differentiated by the fact
that what the burgeoning clouds bequeathed to us
was not death but Oldsmobiles and wall-to-wall shag,
family sitcoms, Rock Hudson melodramas,
Quisp and Quake and Shake 'n Bake. I'm talking about m-m-
my generation, aprés-Boomers and Watergate babies,
vassals of Dumbo, victims of disco, Disney's demented
suburban spawn held in thrall by Herbie the Love Bug
and Dan'l Boone and frozen dinners in the family room.
For his is the land of Salisbury steak and crinkle-cut fries,
his the encampment holding hostage our dreams,
his the painted desert toward which an ever younger legion
flies to fight and die willingly among the ruins
littered with no plastic cactus. Poor, lost Los Angeles.
Fifty years since the war invented the automobile and it
keeps spreading like an oil slick or fungus,
some deviant flora or insect brood corrupt with radiation,

the *Things* and *Its* our fear became those first flush years
of the atomic age. Amazing, this vista, the miles we've logged
from the very first split-levels and miracle appliances,
Levittown to Orange County, the mouse-eared multitude
inching into adolescence as the great consensus waned,
Perry Como supplanted by Elvis, Route 66 replaced by I-40,
Interstates invented by Ike to match the autobahns
he bombed to rubble. And the 60s were born with a whole
lot of shaking and died in the trip wires of Tet,
the 70s churned in a funky inferno—*burn, baby, burn*—
lost souls in sandals and government scandals
preempting the "Brady Bunch" and "Patridge Family,"
and soon they'll be enshrining the 80s
like the happy daze of the 50s before them
as a fun-loving decade of armed intervention and capital gains
overseen by a firm but avuncular Cold Warrior,
a smiling Sandman smelting our stolen ideals to slag.
Burn, baby. Burn. But what will we do for entertainment
now that Uncle Walt is gone, Elvis has left the building,
even the Commies have thrown in the towel?
Where can we turn for self-definition if Lookinglass has landed,
Iron Felix fallen, the Titan of the Carpathians
crumbled to chalk on the Victory of Socialism boulevard?
We've invested so much in World War III it seems a shame
to miss it, killer satellites and high-tech graphics
to grid the incoming contrails, feral survivors
roaming the wasteland in jacked-up desert dune buggies.
For those reared in the shadow of the Fat Man
anything less than global thermonuclear destruction
seems laughable, wimpy, unrealistically naive.

I couldn't begin to count the versions of Armageddon
cast up like driftwood on the shallow bar of my youth:
gamma waves and bacterial plagues, deep space visitations,
killer rabbits run amok in *Night of the Lepus.*
No screenplay apocalypse, no scenario for world holocaust
could fail to provide me with suitable amusement.
The greenhouse effect? Let's grow oranges in Alaska!
Nuclear winter? We'll wear fur coats!
How many Saturdays did I roam the solitude of Rock Creek Park
whacking the heads from the carpet of May apples
that rose like miniature mushroom people from the loam each spring,
the last man left alive, alone with my trusty radio,
stockpiled Spaghetti-Os, and Raquel Welch in her mink bikini.
My favorite survivalist parable was that classic of the genre,
the *Omega Man:* Charlton Heston as a macho scientist
marooned in a barbed-wire penthouse bastion
while the devious albino minions of Brother Matthias essay
to toast him like a cheesepuff with their flaming catapult.
To a battalion of prepubescent fifth-grade boys
assembled on my birthday for pizza and then a movie
at the military hospital where my father saw patients
its peculiar logic was irresistible—wandering the streets
of the virus-riddled city, submachine gun in hand,
torching the cowled and cowering enemy, looting at will
from abandoned stores in a consumerist fantasy spree.
Even the recovering soldiers back from Hue and Da Nang
napalmed hairless as rubber lobsters strolling the lobby
in mint-green sanitary gowns during intermission
couldn't dim our heroic bloodlust. Eventually, of course,
the bad guys contrive to harpoon unlucky Charlton

in a fountain, Ahab and the whale rolled into one,
his blood embodying a second chance for the hippie kids
who must repopulate the planet, a vaccine in the sacristy,
a red sea he might have parted against Pharaoh
in a more familiar role, but it isn't that easy this time, Moses,
I mean Chuck, for we have met the enemy and they
seem more than a little familiar. Surprise! It's us.
You and me and Charlton Heston. As climaxes go,
this is a serviceable, if moralistic, war-horse,
an invocation of divine reckoning gaveled from on high
by the supreme arbiter of truth and justice who remains,
for contractual reasons, off camera. For our purposes
such traditional iconography is entirely unsuited.
We must don the body-armor of secular materialism
to probe the minefields of the Age of Relativity,
though still our animist soul peeks through
in the totem bulls and bears of Wall Street,
the buffalo at Fermilab, the parakeets at Woolworth's,
the way water draws us from the parched interior
to cluster in postmetropolitan conurbations
gridlocked at the edge of the Great Lakes and oceans.
Isn't this another possible ending, a slambang finale
for the movie our search for existential meaning has become,
the gathering-together-of-the-folk-on-the-beach,
a millennial hootenanny of ludic glee, a redemptive conclave
where the blinds and baffles that divide us wash away
while the mother ship announces its queenly ascension
from its secret UFO base beneath the Bermuda Triangle
with the sis-boom-bah anthem of universal kinship?
But does anyone remember the words to that chestnut?

And if we take the sea as our symbol for spiritual longing
have we reduced the human comedy to a beach party flick,
spring break in Fort Lauderdale with Frankie and Annette,
Elvis on board for the making of *Fun in Acapulco?*
Is the theme of salvation even faithful to the script?
Is today's viewing audience likely to credit the trope
of an unseen Canaan on a Hollywood back-lot
toward which Chuck Heston would lead us?
We could close with a medley of our greatest hits,
hula hoops to Indian bingo, pinball machines and mechanical hearts,
protest rallies, rocket launches, traffic jams, swap meets.
But montage is a throwback to the golden age of Tinseltown,
and we've seen those cheesy newsreels a thousand times.
Our final act should be caged in a more contemporary idiom,
sure, postmodern, postindustrial, post-Ford, Post Toasties,
a mise-en-scène more in keeping with the zeitgeist,
the end-of-the-millennium implication of closure
which could lead us on a journey to the great hereafter,
the wild blue yonder, the sweet bye-and-bye,
heaven and hell rolled into one brazenly illumined limbo,
the collective Purgatorio of America's Century,
where the spirits of the departed compose a fluid societal matrix
embracing freedom of expression and laissez-faire economics,
democratic, nonsectarian, centrally air-conditioned,
lacking only a sense of higher purpose—altruism, *civitas,*
the numinous, the sacred—an eternal Las Vegas of the soul,
complete with keno parlors and fast-food franchises,
laundromats and mobile homes and glassy office parks,
a necropolis populated with lonely souls of all descriptions
drinking 7-11 coffee on the way to work,

a mosaic we could tile with the pearl and ebony tesserae
of our favorite cultural icons, JFK and LBJ,
Lucy Ricardo and Charlie Parker, Malcolm X
teaching self-empowerment at the local community college,
Speed Racer hunkered down in the grease pit at Jiffy Lube,
John Belushi playing the slots, Sylvia Plath perambulating Wal-Mart
for jumbo packs of Pampers, the self-destroying angels,
we could make a suburb of their deaths: the Blue Deuce Lounge,
where Hank Williams and Janis Joplin torch a plaintive duet
while Marilyn and James Dean slow dance in the dark;
Kerouac's Bar & Grill; Anne Sexton's Brake & Muffler;
Jarrell & O'Hara's Body Shop and Custom Re-
Finishing—Jackson Pollock is out back right now
air-brushing Chinese dragons on a baby-blue conversion van.
We could borrow that van and cruise the Strip at twilight
with all the beautiful, lost, 27-year-old rock and rollers,
Morrison and Hendrix, Buddy Holly and the rest,
the vomit-choked, the chopper-spavined, the shot-down-in-flames.
We could drive the linear palm-lined boulevards
among the immaculate golf courses and planned communities'
manicured lawns, pastel intaglio wavering at poolside,
TVs dreaming of snow in the darkened living rooms.
We could enter the arc-lit freeway slipstream
and climb the desolate escarpments to the higher desert.
We could travel for miles before stopping by the side of the road,
to stretch our legs, and walk out among the Joshua trees
the suicides are lucky enough to become. At the edge
of the plateau, before looking down at the city
sprawled like a uranium nebula in its inhospitable cradle,
we could pause. We could wait there, hands in pockets,

engine running, with the veiled fire flooding over the rise to etch,
among the creosote and sage, a kind of frenzied hieroglyphic,
the projection of a vast, untranslatable energy
against the furrows of dust as pale and frangible as ash.

TWO FIGURES WITH HEAT LIGHTNING IN THE SANGRE DE CRISTO MOUNTAINS

1

When lightning flashes up a dry mountain valley,
completely without sound but tangible as electricity,
the world stands revealed with the clarity

of raw voltage: the grove of dead pines, bare as toothpicks,
limned in blue fire; the sawblade spine and ribs of rock;
one axe; two pairs of boots; a lone tin can, charred black;

the ring of stones around still-glowing embers
where a half-burned Rice-A-Roni box bears
the preternatural image of a San Francisco cable car.

2

The storm is beautiful. Hiss and whistle of static
discharge in the meadow grass, the plastic
shiver of their tent alive with galvanic sparks

as thunder crests the ridge and runs downstream,
like horses rumbling through the valley, but still no rain.
In this light all scale is lost. Angles and planes

kaleidoscope to nothing. Mercurial tentacles probe earthward,
convulsing into jagged bolts as if the night were
some colossal forge or foundry, a blast furnace where

giant smiths wield red-hot tongs and gunmetal hammers
clang against the anvil, thunder now stammering
over rimrock. As if it were an oceanic hemisphere,

a liquid full of luminous matter assembled like shoals
of plankton or krill, charged particles climbing in spirals,
assuming the double helix of galaxies and cells,

like a souvenir paperweight from New York City,
a miniature blizzard encircling the captive totem of liberty,
pollen-storm of plastic specks engulfing her tiny

torch and body within. As if two figures with heat lightning
in the Sangre de Cristo mountains were something
other than motes of a particular place and time, anything

more than dust suspended in that high alpine vale.
Now the lightning comes at longer intervals,
the tall grass thrashes less. The splintered light reveals

the columbines' ruby crescendo subside to an almost
perfect calm. Moon-shadows cloak the talus slope
as the storm moves off, southwest, toward Alamosa.

3

At dawn they rise to break camp before breakfast.
They drink strong coffee, crouch on their heels to eat
dried apricots and raisins mixed with cream of wheat.

Above the ridge the sky is already blue and full
of clouds like Spanish galleons under sail.
They douse the fire and set out along the trail.

By noon the valley is far behind them.

ROCK FALLS, ILLINOIS

Now the clouds are pleasure craft and tugboats towing strings of empties
    across the mighty Mississippi.
Now we're singing "Ring of Fire" as we slough past scrapwood shacks
    strung high along the levee,
regiments of willow shoots, phalanxes of cottonwood among the islets and
    sandy channels,
backwater mudflats papered in drowned nilotic reeds with seedpods
    rattling in empty sockets
like Babylonian baby toys, like the stork and ibis amulets of ancient
    Sumerian funerary wands.
Now the palisades are waving kindled branches in warning. Now the local
    flocks: crow, duck, grackle.
Now the night has shed its skin and taken root, alluvial soil two hundred
    feet deep, black earth overturned
as the ungainly reapers ratcheting dry stalks to husk-mulch and grain clip
    by in the dusty acres of sheaves.
Now Patty Loveless is on the radio. Now the annual interstate game with
    the ritual rival across the river.
Now squadrons of geese settle to the stubble field, bushels of apples and
    butternut squash,
hay bales, clover honey, scarecrows bearing pumpkins and cider to
    scavenge the empty miles of silos.
Now the country music station from DeKalb or Clinton begins to falter as
    we come to the first sure sign of the city,

road deconstruction, cigarettes and lotto tickets, two lanes of
    jackhammered arterial funnel
to choke the reek of mini-marts and muffler shops back to the long-
    corrupted aorta.
Now the mills like skeletons of prehistoric whales in the distance.
Now the familiar planetary gloom of a pancake house orbiting against
    ectopic eclipse,
waiters trundling gurneys of blueberry syrup like doctors delivering a
    miracle serum
to the lone patient left alive inside the Belgian waffle ward. Now the old
    neighborhoods of the millworkers,
blue-domed churches and backyard shrines, shuttered taverns and Union
    Halls,
blocks of wooden bungalows with Old World flags and used car dealers
    flying patriotic bunting.
Now the upturned cobbles are cast against the ice machine behind the
    liquor store.
Now the country music is lost altogether. Now we too are lost among the
    mills and foundries collapsing in decay,
brickyards and crucibles, husks the size of aircraft hangars full of desolate
    machinery
like the ruins of ancient siege engines or prized displays at a trade show or
    ghostly exhibition,
the Great Hall of Abandoned Dreams. Now the road expires in barbed wire
    and tangled thickets,
the bridge a ruin of joists and wishbones in the weeds and broken cinder
    blocks below,
the Rock River rife with trash and spoil like an animal slit open by hunters
    to spill the foam and spoor of its entrails.

Now the forsaken freight tracks lead nowhere. Now grocery carts are
    wheeled across the empty lots
by the hands of invisible shoppers gloved in fallen leaves. Now the clouds
    are barges full of salt.

DAWN

A man and a woman are driving across the Great Plains of North America.

Kansas. Saskatchewan. South Dakota.

They are hundreds of miles into their journey, cocooned by speed and metal and dusk, a chrysalis of solitude and cobalt distance. They are bodiless and encapsulated as astronauts approaching the moons of Jupiter,

their radio emits a voice-storm of signals and significant noise,

by the dashboard light they can just make out the markings on the map, a grave-rubbing or ghostly palimpsest,

scrim as fine as angel's hair or the latticed veins of tangerines,

images and symbols which admit of no single probable answer but function as a kind of orchestral score for the landscape sweeping invisibly past,

a notational logic of the possible.

Hiss of tires, rush of wind, cardinal hush and ordinal thrum.

Toward dawn the radio begins another cycle.

Everything is exactly as it was. They have outdistanced the stars and the plains are just as silent, gravid, ineluctable. They have received the hieratic lunar mysteries, they possess the blueprints of a thousand civilizations.

They stop the car and get out.

In the first, ashen light shapes and templates begin to appear.

A horse, a flock of doves, windrows of trees between the freshly plowed fields, distant cathedrals of grain elevators rising from the mist.

They have everything they need to create the world.

They have only to join hands. They have only to choose.

AT THE FREUD HILTON

Sturm und Drang narcissus, loose petals
in the windstorm of love: thus the anonymous
supplicants at the bus stop
across from the zoo

wait to see their analysts before work,
patient as jonquils beneath yellow umbrellas,
these brothers and sisters
in loneliness. In tranquil offices they will recall

the stuff of dreams, read the palm
of memory's hand, explore the polar regions
with a rush of self-realization
and the grace to give way

to warmer currents. This is how
the city was built: blueprints and jackhammers,
hard hats eating tuna sandwiches
exist, but only as so much flotsam in the backwash,

it is these galoshes-wearing islands
that form the more than token
archipelago of the resident, grief-stricken
here and now. Egrets,

dawn visions from some wild-eyed goddess of the Euphrates,
rise dimly from the heron house.
Reptiles, small mammals, the greater and lesser
numberings of the swarm.

Commuters gearing up for the day's multifarious
faces, ranks of polished coins, reflections
tossed from window to window
of a passing bus.

SHRIMP BOATS, BILOXI

These wings, these lights, this shoal of angels
sieved against the gulf, gull-bent
arks of the high dusk
waters, arm in arm, rippled and linked
in their slow patrol
and orbit, the fleet, the nets,
the numerals
from which our days evolve,
wave-battered, moon-betrayed, fluid
as silk. Still
the moment
impends. A father and son
are trolling the shallows
for mullet, knee-deep beneath the pillared
dream of the interstate engineers
at neap tide. The black-
jacketed Baptists down from the convention
center for coffee and fried
oysters preach amazing
grace the gospel of life hereafter
as they distribute
refrigerator
magnets, but those who attend
the keening dorsals

are none so
certain, I mean the dolphins'
jeremiad, milky tiger
lilies speaking in tongues, wind-shuck
of the exhausted flocks, oil
rigs and pelicans and harbor-craft
on Mobile Bay, shiver
and rock
of the voyage out,
the journey
in, I mean
the rage of faith,
I mean the light-storm, blind
drunk on the oceanic
surge, I mean
the jerks, the shakes, the waves'
lupercalia,
the blue seizures
of noon. Sweet
sugar of life
deliver me the means
to fix, grant me the music,
the salt, the song. Vast rapture of this world
bear me with the wings and candles
of your chosen
vessels, number me
among that company,
raise me high upon your darkening
harmony. Tide, wind, spirit
take me up
in these rags of twilight.

ODE TO THE WILD HORSES OF CAINEVILLE, UTAH

I don't remember where we first found mention of them,
what offbeat billboard or cheap travel guide,
what tourist brochure perused over cold lobby java and unsugared sinkers
at the Gallup Econolodge or Barry's Blue Mesa Motel,
but we never could find it again, not one word,
though we plundered our trove of informational flotsam
with reckless abandon, pored through the jumble of triple-A maps,
ransacked the *Road Atlas* page by weary page.
Elizabeth says it must have been the placemats
where we ate those Navajo tacos for dinner in Bluff;
they were depicted as local "Creatures of Legend,"
along with the Gila monster and high mountain cougar,
silver fox and golden eagle, even the lowly seagull,
which carries a certain weight in these parts,
in memory of that miraculous flock which saved the first crop
from the cricket plague, a providential portent of divine approbation,
not to mention a free demonstration of the great salt Zion's
practicability. *Avis ex machina,* a serious omen.
For our part, we followed the only signs we knew,
state highway markers cast as black-and-white beehives,
a rust-and-buckshot desert apiary, lonely sentinels
along those rudderless, earth-woven roads.
Leaving Bluff at dawn we struck for the interior
and it was as if we had fallen asleep to the cries of owls

or the musical sky beneath the Owachomo natural bridge
and dreamed it all, dreamed our life as this journey
through gardens and ossuaries of wind,
choirs enthroned in the arches and marrowbones,
song-shape, unnameable stone, neck of a swan or violin;
or else it was a movie, dreamlike and incantatory
swirl of images across the screen as we halve the abyss
and rise to cedar breaks and trembling aspens at altitude,
black rock, red rock, dolly to the switchback,
zoom to the impossible azure-fingered vision of Lake Powell,
toward whose heart we dive in our underwear,
piercing the water's turquoise flesh, seeking the sunken
Anasazi realm of moss and monkeyflowers
on the lost canyon floor.
                    Then the unweaving:
        cut from the hills to the interstate at St. George,
into the Virgin River gorge,
            mule deer assembled at the water's edge,
        trucks on the freeway in violet dusk,
                dancers enraptured
    with perpetual motion.
                        It seemed we drove forever,
twenty hours at least. I remember we saw two rooster-tailed comets
before crossing the last ridge to Las Vegas
and wondered if they could outshine the neon galaxies
of the Stardust, out-glitter the Gulch's bulbed utopia.
We slept at a Travelodge behind the Tropicana
and in the morning burned the last, sun-blasted miles to L.A.,
where the communion of that day was leached by the sprawl
of freeways and friends, Tommy Burgers, Long Beach,

the talking walrus at Universal Studios,
weeks of driving still to come:

                        glaciers and missile silos,
          grey whales and cheese dogs,
the Finnish-American Labor Halls of Astoria
         and the Million Dollar Cowboy Bar in Jackson Hole,
             Mendocino and Seattle,
           Twodot and Revelstoke,
   the sorrowful beauty of Richard Hugo country
             and South Dakota's insidious array,
        Wall Drug and Mount Rushmore,
      the Corn Palace at Mitchell,
        the Passion Play at Spearfish
         we can only imagine,
      Jesus of the Badlands,
Jesus of the Black Hills arise!
           Rose we did.
And shone, and drove. We rolled to the rhythm of the open road,
grooved the straightaways on cruise control,
climbed to the heights without stripping the gears,
paused at the peak of the pass and just hung there,
imperturbably paired, like condors.
What freedom we felt on those thermals and updrafts,
the highway's empty miles and serendipitous gyres,
the nation's extravagant beauty and materialistic soul,
not so much a movable feast as a smorgasbord on wheels,
happy hour refills and bottomless cups of joe,
all you can eat for one low price:
            prime rib in Missoula,
              Hunan in Vancouver,

biscuits and gravy and grits in Biloxi,
                Frosted Pop-Tarts in the Tuolumne meadows,
sweet Rainier cherries in the shadow of Mount Shasta,
                fresh corn roasted in the coals
                        with a solid chardonnay
                in aluminum cups
                        or a pizza in the room
                at the Motel 6,
        falling asleep to lake-light of Orion
or the late-night surf report on ESPN.
                                Lo,
our wheels clicked and spun with the rattle of dice,
the days conspired to yield a palpable balm as fine as basswood honey,
as true a token as the fever dreams vouchsafed to certain
ascetic sects through divine revelation or trial by fire
and driving Utah is a little of each. Elizabeth,
I've dreamt my life a thousand times in a thousand ways,
a favorite film with multiple endings, the many journeys
that make up the one, and you are the star of each,
the ubiquitous heroine on the Stardust marquee,
the constellation by which I sight, though even on occluded nights
I can detect your polar inference, as Harriet Tubman
felt her way to freedom by the mossy sides of trees.
Faith, they say, is blind,
                        but there are always signs:
                even Brigham Young had read John C. Fremont,
        heard the mountain trappers tell of tall grass waving
in the rain-rich shadow of the Wasatch Range;
        John Wesley Powell descended the impassable Colorado
                because the laws of science demanded it;

compiled ethnological data and mastered the local lingo;
devised systems of land classification and water distribution;
surveyed, plotted, theorized, mapped—
this as a one-armed veteran of Shiloh,
a man who during the siege of Vicksburg
took time from his command in the Illinois artillery
to search the earthworks and mortar-torn trenches
for fossils.
Such is the force of belief;
such the hunger for indisputable evidence.
So too beneath these catalogues there lies a buried essence,
a brass ring or trilobite, a golden coin
in the wedding cake of tiers and geological strata,
though finding it may be like digging for bones
in the wide flesh of the oceans, as hard to pin down
as the Henry Mountains in midsummer heat shimmer,
like tracing the clouds or our precise route
that day out of Bluff, impossible, but it's there,
I can feel it like a lodestone, and I know
that it's you. I almost forgot the wild horses.
At first we caught their smell, a salt and metal musk
sour as nickels along the Fremont River,
just outside of town. And then, rounding a bend,
the road was a riot of roans and pintos
and palomino stallions rearing through the cloud,
dust and flies and sandy flanks,
the clamor of the remuda in full flight around us.
It only took a moment to realize our mistake.
Cows. Cattle. A boisterous herd driven to pasture
by three blonde cowgirls on chestnut mares,

young girls in jeans and lipstick frosted
pink as the denizens of any suburban mall.
It seemed a perfect demystifying parable,
but our hearts were too full, the day too beautiful.
When the grit had settled and the mooing stopped
and we rolled into Caineville for milkshakes and gas,
the man at the Texaco told us there were no horses,
it must have been some kind of hoax,
he'd lived his whole life there and never seen one.
He was quite vehement, smeared with grease,
intent that we should grant his point.
We did. Of course there are no horses,
certainly, of course. But what does it matter?
This is a love story, not a western.